HOLISTIC COLLABORATION
Series - Presents Book #1:

CONNECTING
POETRY

Body and Soul Nutrition

By
SHERRY BAINBRIDGE, PhD

HOLISTIC COLLABORATION Series:

Connecting Poetry - Body and Soul Nutrition
by Sherry Bainbridge

Copyright © 2019 HOLISTIC COLLABORATION

https://holisticcollaboration.com

Table of Contents

INTRODUCTION

(Please Note: ***** means this word is in the
Definition section – page 82.)

The Poetry Connection presents a few standards
in human-kind personality that support our own
ability to communicate with *energy/spirit. It
offers thought in connecting with ourselves and,
thereby, gaining experience in communicating
with spiritual guidance. They consider how to
lovingly *align thinking with emotion, thought,
and *feelings. This is how to become compatible
with our own ability to tell truth, *heal, influence,
and create life. It is what I believe, work at, and
live every day. It starts with the individual. If
more of us are doing the same, then like energy
creates and expands.

By trade, curiosity, and necessity: I am a
Naturopathic (Holistic Health Doctor),
Hypnotherapist, Medical/Spiritual Intuitive, and
Reiki Master/Teacher. A formal and self-
education in Eastern, Western, and Tribal healing
and spiritual philosophies. It is always a collection
of people, thoughts, and efforts that are needed
to achieve anything. It is a Holistic Collaboration
of the physical and the divine.

1

This life-view leads to being more adaptable, truth-aware, confident, calmer, healthier, active, less resistant, and aids in developing faith and trust in spirit and ourselves. It is a flexible foundation for increasing the right confidents, balance, is humbling, helpful, increases laughter, eases stress, and in time develops wisdom. All highly nutritional for the body and the *soul.

*God/energy/spirit/vibration is unfailing in its accuracy and guidance. It brings life-altering experiences and insights. Provides endless opportunities to grow and, sometimes to just be, observe, and to allow things to unfold without any interference. Spirit guides us in what to do, when to do, how to do, and if to do. It exposes truth! It is the master instructor for lining up, at the same time; emotion, feeling, and thinking with the true essence of the heart. This is 'balance'. It is in this state that healing miracles and life *manifestation are set into motion.

As for the writing of the poetry – WHO KNEW! I have never been into poetry, so when I started putting my perspective in this concise yet artistic format, I was more shocked and challenged than anyone could imagine. I guess if I can write poetry, then writing like a normal person should be easier, right? It has been a brutal, exciting, humbling, and personally healing experience. It has given me *hope* for the future.

The greatest blessing of all for me is the opportunity to share something that may ease someone else's life – as so many frequently and generously do for mine! I guarantee I will learn more from you. It always works this way, and, for this, I am deeply honored and thank you ahead of time.

Luckily, spirit is not always serious. Like humans, energy can be incredibly entertaining and humorous.   Laughter is healing for the beings capable. For this reason, the character 'Nog,' the What Blah, was designed to lighten things up a bit. The Holistic Collaboration series also offers a YouTube show every Tuesday: **Peeves, Tips, and Tricks.**   This will share a variety of fun and educational insights for holistic living. Including personal approaches and experiences.

Will you please join with Holistic Collaboration as we respectfully strive to regain our birthright and most powerful resource – loving connection!

Thank you for reading on.

Disclaimer: Please insure that you always involve your licensed mental and health professionals before making any drastic life changes. None of this is in replacement of their good advice and participation.

HOW THIS BOOK CAME ABOUT

The first seed of the Holistic Collaboration series started decades ago: I died! At 9 years old I had 3 serious infections. I remember floating about in spirit form above a fever-induced unconscious body many times. I had been seriously Ill for over 2 weeks. One time, I heard what I thought would be help walking down the hallway. I zipped back into my physical form. The person cracked open the door, poked their head in, and assumed I was sleeping and quickly closed the door. At that moment I fell into the depths of hopeless emotions. My energy-body went down through the physical, around to the left, stood up and stepped right in front of several very tall beings. It was nothing, easy, familiar, I was never afraid or even questioned.

The beings stated that they were concerned about my not meeting my purpose and explained why. They gave me a choice to stay or come back. In that extremely brief moment, I considered a couple things, then I felt the strength and courage in my spirit begin to rise. The next thought was; "I think I can." Boom, I was back! Within the hour I started recovering. It was validating and life-altering.

I decided to find ways to heal at every level possible; to be deeply genuine, honest, and reasonably self-sufficient. To resolve ongoing healing, strive for excellence, and by doing so, make it easier on others by sharing whatever possible. Nothing like a little self-inflicted pressure! But now, in these times, I find the knowledge and skills learned so far, are irreplaceable and priceless!

It is my vision to help people embrace and elevate the beauty and guidance in emotion as a gift to be cherished not shut down. To meet and join with others also striving to create a better world.

This is a time to get excited! We *share* this world. There is no fight, it is a state of acceptance, be-ing, and like-mindedness that gives strength to change. We are, after all, 90% energy. I believe the poems share ways to be compatible with, and to take advantage of the power in *light, to influence life.

And so, the creation of the Holistic Collaboration series' 1st book: The Poetry Connection. I hope you like it.

A HOLISTIC COLLABORATION

Changing the state of things requires that
  different is done.
We are all experts in resisting and struggling
  with this one.
There is much good and knowledge available to
  those on earth,
To aid and guide all in this repetitive and
  challenging place to traverse.

The poetry within these pages are exactly how I
  try to live and think.
Earned by many efforts and mistakes, they are
  my daily blueprint.
There are many before and here making a great
  difference for all of humanity.
I am humbled and in awe with all the efforts in
  averting further insanity.

Holistic living is seeing all potential influential
   factors explored or not, seen and unseen.
In collaborating we can help each other reach
   higher states to better handle many extremes.
In a lifetime of study in collective and self-
   connection restoration,
I gratefully have been led to the birthing of
   Holistic Collaboration.

ADDICTIVE EARTH

Humanity is consumed with the artistry of addiction
Vehemently holding onto this subject with conviction.
Addicted to healthful nutrition, hydration, and air…
Or being bitchy, controlling, negative… so beware;

The coiling struggle with the absence of self-control,
Compromises integrity, *well-being, and takes a toll.

Creating justified *sociopathic behaviors like
  lying, manipulation...
Undermining the soul and putting quality and
  trust into question.

Concealing and living in an illusion that one day
  will cause suffering,
Forgetting the gift of common sense and
  succumbing to self-buffering.
A cheater's way to unmask a different self-
  version.
Bypassing earning the skills found in kind self-
  assertion.

There is a high price to pay for self and external
  swindling.
Squandering genuine inner-guidance excels
  reality dwindling.
It bridles external expression.
Hazing subjective impressions.

Energy struggles to mentor through the numbed
  senses.
Retracting itself organically, intensifying life's
  disturbances.
A spiritual effort to get attention
Focused on unresolved inner tensions.

Feelings are scrambled and misarranged.
Clarity and growth are then exchanged.
As various regulators await within to aid
In communicating; "why we are afraid!"

Trapped in further numbing to soften the
  harshness of contradictive battling.
An unhealthy escape that clouds the mind and
  heart, exchanging them for self-stonewalling.
It disintegrates the progress and skills that lead
  to graceful and kind life-connections.
Where courage, compassion, and thought
  exercises detailed life navigation.

The *higher self and energy support us in
  advancing;
Not in being *closed-minded, immobile, or
  backtracking.
Even nature and science move forward,
As this is the way the universe is ordered.

Stop resisting that which you already know.
Be, do and think differently and learn to let go.
Get excited and embrace the virtue in change,
To align life with more progress and less pain.

Of course, this is easier said than done,
Requiring uncomfortable love for the one.

Educating, identifying, trusting, and
  comprehending this energetic communication
  removes friction.
It will simplify understanding its guidance so it
  can assist in healthier connections; the only
  way to cure addiction!

THE BETWEEN SPACE OF SURRENDER

Standing once again in the *between.
Not sure which way is best to turn.
It is here where we gently lean
On the skill of presence to discern.

Just wait, just wait, quietly. Do not try to force.
Be still, silent, listen, alert yet free from thought.
Absorbing, observing, open to all on this course.
Wisdom is earned in this most sacred *Akashi
  spot.

Pressed amid that which is new and the choices
  of the past,
There is no escape from the push and pull of this
  place.

*Kinetically, it mentors the execution of each
  intended task.
For now, remain quiet, just be, wait, listen, and
  do not fixate.

Guidance is revealed between all words and
  sound.
Life secrets are unlocked here, available for all to
  gain
Insights and directions, lingering patiently to be
  found.
A balancing energetic sway of great beauty and
  pain.

It blends with all that we are, have been, and will
  be.
Ask now for counsel to *gently* come, and refuse
  to derail.
Energy glides to and from this place of the all
  and the *empty.
Providing, to those alert and aware; most every
  needed detail.

This creation cycle brings forth what we need to
  receive.
Facilitating and navigating the motions in this
  physical plane.

Freely offering exactly what is needed for all to
  achieve.
It is beyond the confines of the façade believed
  of time-space.

Spirit pops in and out, both serene and bold,
  taking a solid stance.
It prompts us until we are ready, then executes
  with striking skill.
*Surrendering without fear is how to utilize the
  design of this dance,
As its ultimate prize is a human's most ardent
  desire: A life fulfilled!

DEAFENIZATION

Ear *chakras sit at an angle at the temples,
Dense with energy, altered and disassembled.
Blocked by destructive and inaccurate, mind
  chatter,
Damaged thinking caused by willfully adapted
  patterns.

Forgetting the exquisiteness of life studied
  through listening,
Causing energy stiffness that results in feeble
  deafening.
A sense so very precious,
A loss acutely careless.

Pretending each time,
That speaking is prime.
Evaporating the skill of the attentive,
Taking with it the art of being receptive.

16

Telling each ear, it is not valued, and hearing is
  further lost.
The body rallies, supporting every thought; have
  you forgot?
Such dominate mutterings are not learned by
  coincidence,
A calculated inducement for mortal
  insignificance.

Will you regret not hearing the lies of politicians?
Or maybe the words of manipulating
  statisticians?
Long for the bombardment of commercials,
Or the sound of the intrusive industrials?

Yearn for the swishing sound of a cool breeze
Gently rustling along the length of the leaves?
Perhaps you will miss the rippling and splashing
  of water on the shore,
Or the beauty in hearing increasing acoustics
  before and within a storm?

Possibly, the thrill of the song of a whale,
Or the pleasure heard in one that prevails?
What will you miss after telling your ears?
That they are no longer needed to hear.

ELECTRICAL DATING

Finding love in a disconnected place
Causes quick and narrow appraise.
Where denied dishonesty entraps and retards,
Often crumbling things before they even start.

Many unfamiliar with the skills of internal and
  external communication.
Blindly stumbling about for a chance at
  compatible infatuation.
Unsure of what either will uncover,
As dating has many disguised puzzlers.

The majority fighting the feeling of not being
  good enough,
Yet still hopeful in finding a deserving heart to
  entrust.
All desiring an initial connection detection,
Knowing the overwhelming odds of rejection.

Naturally occurring experiences bring up
  opportunities to learn and overcome,
An effective, keen and streamlined school for
  self-improvement is the way this is done.
It is full of insightful advancements that are
  necessary to broaden smarts
In the search for a special person who ignites all
  the right sparks.

A match that has each doing their part to make
  things brighter
By designing a life alliance outline as a
  participating author.
Becoming what we seek unites life with the mind
  and heart,
And fills it to overflowing, washing away many
  painful scars.

Be useful and change into what you deeply
 desire,
Doing so teaches, demonstrates to others, and
 inspires.
It puts out energy that guides, attracts, and
 supports in response.
Increasing the odds of attracting in, exactly what
 you need and want.

ENERGY NOTES

Spirit is like an orchestra,
A vibrational musical mantra.
It molds life and shifts as it directs,
And has both gentle and harsh effects.

It can be difficult, illusive, simplistic, complicated
and is a highly individualized process.
Energy expands with the frequencies of
vibrations intended towards progress.
We are mostly energy, so understanding this
principal makes total common sense.
As it ultimately allows human beings to set up
our own life-coordinating offense.

Consider that one of the orchestra's violins has a
string out of tune,
This one little thing begins impacting everyone in
the room.
Somehow the musician does not notice,
Lost in remote thought like a musical novice.

The conductor and members become impatient
At the disrespect of someone so complacent.
Continuing on, the audience begins to thin.
Likely not willing to easily return again.

Energy has abundant and very long arms,
Increasing its strength to alter and transform.
It is a functioning, living, spiritual machine
Calibrated for helping Universal manifesting.

Correctly tuned energy attracts, guides and
  interacts.
It brings in that which agrees with thinking, or it
  tries to correct.
The goal is to become fearless in excellence,
Honoring the power of energy with reverence.

This approach opens the expression of emotion
  and creativity.
These are precious and vital gift's in the power of
  connectivity.
Through these, our innate abilities show, and
  then begin to grow,
All because of communicating and acting *with*
  the *energy-flow.

ENERGY TIP 101

Individuals that *bitch* about other people, will
Bitch about the people they bitch with!
They will show how they think
By the way they speak and treat.

THE FALLING OF RELIGION

People mentored and guided by fear, learn not
   to ask many questions.
Sheltering and defending subjective opinions
   with great conviction,
Fervently safeguarding the beliefs of individual
   exalted illumination.
Most never realize the rooted corruption hidden
   near and in the foundations.

Religions of the world are falling,
As God has sent many angels calling.
Meant to separate the truths from the cults,
Shaking and shocking members by default.

Underneath the depths of support lies great evil,
A corruption so thick it has begun to overspill.
It is showing long and deep structural cracks,
Displaying how much spirit religions can lack.

There is no cause to point fingers, guilt, or shame
 good followers.
Everyone has been fooled, more than once, by
 darker influencers.
Accept responsibility, gather, and give strength
 to this collapse
By building an incompatible structure that is
 harder for evil to attack.

Let go of what was previously thought,
And be grateful these sins are finally caught.
Do not engage in such a corrupt and firm battle,
Just leave, don't waste stress and time to haggle.

There are good ideas to keep as we move
 forward,
And charity necessary to help a world so
 disordered.
Let's not forget, amongst these harsh failures,
The great good that was carefully configured.

Lovingly support that which has value and truth,
Harmonizing it, to begin birthing something new.
All need to be a caring, helpful, and loving
 humanity member.
As these are the only way to be in contradiction
 with the sinister.

THE FUNDAMENTALS OF SELF

Often, it seems, that darkness is all around.
Keeping us camouflaged and totally bound.
Confined in the world of a shadowy womb.
Harshly arriving into a most wild classroom.

With expectations of becoming bright and bold.
Shocking, for most, to have forgotten how cold.
Ancient memories and history are corrupted or
  wiped clean,
Impairing senses, knowledge, and darkening our
  gleam.

Forging ahead into uncertain futures as
  evolutional pupils within earth's tutorial,
Meant to overcome barriers and learn powerful
  life-skill rules beyond the instinctive primordial.

This brings to light the laws of the physical, energetic,
And human tenets beyond that of any genetics.

Spirit gently impresses us to stimulate our hearts with revitalized creativity.
Inviting in varies training for knowledge, *expansion, and activities.
Attracting many opportunities that blossom life's abundant potential
That reconnects people to an influential, natural guidance fundamental.

Healthy emotional energy has power and is imperative for establishing hope.
Unhealthy emotion stagnates people in a self-loathing suffocating smoke.
It masks deep pain, denied weakness, and unresolved tears.
Altering its assistance for overcoming disguised and inhibiting fears.

Energy navigates the directions
For everyone's higher education.
Bestowing knowledge for willing human-kind.
It will unravel the buried and historically denied.

Intending us to improve in awareness and
   balance
In its amplifications towards inventive
   deliverance.
It unblocks a purer and more intelligent
   connection with ourselves.
In coming full circle, spirit simply introduces us
   to the real self!

GAUGING THE EGO

Set the *ego aside today.
Love and hug it, then put it away.
It is there if you need to retrieve,
Always around, it will never leave.

Ego waits every moment
For its own amusement.
Ready to lead you adrift.
Inclined to steal your gifts.

Unhindered and undaunted it will abuse.
Anchorless, it will exploit you as its muse.
Damaging with harsh defeating criticisms',
That self-inflict deadly comparison fatalism.

Convinced that it is totally worthless,

And believing it to be thoroughly useless.
Costly and mistaken notions to reevaluate,
As this gauge also has the ability to regulate.

It forces up contradictive emotion,
Scrutinizing the truth of devotion.
It makes visible that which is out-of-line and
 needs to be revised.
Properly used, it is an impressively accurate
 device.

Energy rally's in healthy self-competition.
It is supreme for internal observation.
Be respectful of its vain misleading dangers.
Carefully, honestly, use it only to empower.

GRACEFULLY GREAT

Minds neglected and lives unlived; dismissed,
  waiting to grow old.
Forever bound in strained self-relationships and
  societal molds.
Undermined by repetitious thought limitations.
Reinforced by giving-up on life-participation.

Days begin drifting into the next, each a blur of
  the repeated one before.
Rectifying these imposed-challenges, brings in
  light so life can be restored.
Habits enhancing the mind, body, and spirit in
  broadening *grace;
Is exactly what it takes to become a human that
  is great!

HAPPY BIRTHDAY LOVE

Another year and on this day, <u>45</u> years ago:
A mother and father brought you into grow.
A new generation from a most sacred act.
Lovingly providing much of what is lacked.

Starting a life filled with many trials anew.
Moving forward, you learned and grew.
Into this world a young <u>man</u> was caste.
Muddling through and forming a past.

Gaining knowledge, experience, and scars.
Quickly time passes, and here you are;
<u>Forty-five</u> years of human time.
In awe, it is all so very sublime.

Speckled remnants of history now confirm
That this mature <u>man</u> has greatly learned.
Rising each day to set up for and face the next.
With easy laughter showing how blessed.

The journey is eternal making it all still fresh and
   young.
Regardless of people's ideas, this is how human
   life is done:
Obtaining wisdom every step of the way,
To earn a valued life, each and every day.

And in this most precious moment of truth
(As sweet as the most sugary of fruit);
Love, my dear, is no longer held at bay,
As the gift of love is finally here to stay.

HAPPY BIRTHDAY

Note: Change age and gender to personalize

HAPPY MOTHER'S DAY STEPMOM

I have a second mom that is so special,
She gives of her heart so caringly artful.
Filled with love, she wraps me up,
Like a precious treasured buttercup.
I am grateful to have this second chance
To have a mom with love so enhanced!

Thank you, Happy Mother's Day – Love you

HELLO? IS ANYONE LISTENING?

It matters not the before, after, or uncommon
But how we traverse the ground we are on.
Sincerely, thank you to all those out there,
Uniquely experiencing with great self-care.

Confirming, enlightening, transforming beliefs,
Teaching each other from somewhere very deep.
Viewing life the same, would bore many to tears.
Keeping us stuck in a slow and clogged gear.

Examining advantages, challenges, and stumbles
  along the way.
Witnessing each other in how to, or how not to,
  live another day.
While watching each other; I think we would like
  to see,
A world of ingenuity, mutual respect, and
  harmony agreed.

Inducing this place to turn around,
Laughter and peace would abound.
Where dreams and life could grow in health,
And honesty is considered the highest of wealth.

I ASKED; THE TREE ANSWERED

Today I am sitting in front of a beautiful tree,
Totally wrapped up and consumed with me.
Relaxing in the sun shining warm and bright,
Breathing in as the beauty envelopes my sight.

I kindly ask the tree to share its wisdom with me,
And am listening for its words very carefully.
Diffusing my consuming thoughts, I begin to
  pray.
Peacefulness floods in, dispelling emotional
  decay.

The tree speaks; "Stop focusing on past events,
Wasting time worrying about the present,
And fearing the very future you create.
Confront and alter every sabotaging trait.

Change until you see that you are your hope;
You are your success and the ability to cope.
Healing from the inside out, makes for the
  strongest of skin,
No pretenses, just genuineness and courage to
  face what's within.

Shed impairing self-realisms to expose
  uncomfortable vulnerability,
As this is the guide to reconcile disabling wounds
  blocking tranquility.
Emotion helps by divulging the things that must
  be faced,
Bubbling and rising up, buried within the dirt of
  this place.

Denial nurtures strong roots and increases the
  depths of stagnation.
Dangerously lowering energy and its protective
  vibrations.
Trust and faith will ease the challenges within
  these generous learning opportunities.
Authentic sincerity is the threshold to a more
  accurate outer and inner-reality.

Bravely seek out the more profound higher-self,
For within this, lays a lush garden full of wealth.

Systematically tear down all sickly comparison
  fences,
To free radiance and liberate conflicting internal
  clashes.

Be flexible; alert; fluctuating with the *all-
  possibilities* of life,
And continue to restructure thought; these are
  the paths of the wise.
Set aside the faulty ego and observe with an
  open heart and mind.
Nature really is *enlightened, timeless, and
  totally entwined."

A bit stunned as the tree diffused every one of
  my reservations
With clarity, communication, and
  straightforward revelations.
"Take hold of all your life and remember these
  words well,
Because these *etheric roots; are to keep you
  from living in hell."

INTERTWINING HEARTS

We are what romantic dreams and love fantasies
  are all about.
Joining in another destiny with someone known
  from times before.
Deep in the essence of the heart, the soul steps
  up to shout out:
"Fearlessly venture forward into the unknown,
  allow love to transform."

We have met many times before to repeat a
  pattern that ends in both taking flight.
A familiar script like those written into a soap
  opera with a dramatic heartfelt flare,
Where the romancing character scenarios
  separate only to once again reunite.
A consistent friendship over time; an
  unbreakable connection forever shared.

Natural learning is a challenging teacher here
  and can leave many in dismay.
It is no wonder there are so many perceived
  barricades blocking such repairs.

But therein lies the answer; the power in
  embracing perpetual growths passageway.
Requiring each to join in life and inspiring inner-
  observation towards removing snares.

Sensitive love can be so frightening when
  present views are based on past fates.
History influences and can darken the now, but it
  does not formulate future horizons.
It starts with a choice; a single decision; an
  energetic permission to open love's gate.
Unifying it with the power in the energetic
  stream within love and bonding celebrations.

Sprouting adoration is a treasure, a welcome
  deliverance,
A delightful distraction interweaving us in many
  ways.
It goes beyond this life, and this specific
  experience.
But again, duplicating patterns begin to drive this
  love away.

Continuing to betray the gateways we have
  faced together,
Steadfastly holding on to old restricting love
  impressions.

Quietly endorsing each and every disappearing
  layer.
Secretly reinforcing the other's unuttered
  rejections.

Tightly closed doors of the heart, results in love
  moving and shifting out of reach.
Ransacking the likelihood of an exquisitely
  fulfilling, and caring connection.
The heart becomes suppressed, blocking
  awareness so, it no longer is able to teach.
Optimism fades, then steps aside, hesitant and
  unwilling to nurture love's progressive motion.

A familiar relationship repetition that isolates,
  making room for just one.
Emotion rises, altering the energies, mirroring
  the image of self-imposed bias.
Confused, unamused, carrying with it the
  familiar sting of grief in being alone.
I wonder what it would be like, deep in the
  loveliness of dreams, to end this chaos.

New paths begin to emerge, revealing and
  directing through this transition,
Complicated by vulnerable insecurities that stifle
  each heart and soul.

This instills gripping fear of the unknown and its
  unfinished canvass of creation.
Longing then begins sealing off the heart's
  loneliest, darkest, and emptiest holes.

This causes emotional and physical suffering, in
  the unfulfilled yearnings of desire.
It securely shelters the treasures, concealing
  them behind induced obstructions.
Ego quickly takes over, building denial and
  perceptions that set love aside.
Choosing to fairly and honestly face ourselves, is
  how to initiate life reconstructing.

Time will then begin to move forward more
  rapidly than before.
Current memories will grow strong as old stories
  are soon foregone.
New opportunities start to arise, firmly closing
  this tattered door.
The capacity to reopen it is gone, and finally, life
  has moved on.

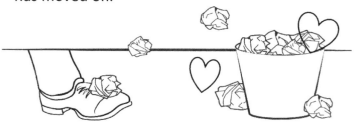

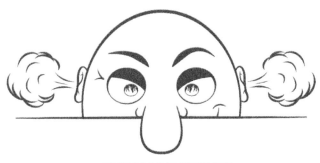

THE LIARS' TOWER

Highly damaging and habitual to Human Nature
Is exaggerating, it is a most destructive danger.
It continues to undermine all of humankind,
And always is crafted in preconceived designs.

Willful falsehoods are crafted and painted.
Knowledge omitted and selfishly fragmented,
Forming a world based on the power of lying,
As mistrust and division for each keep rising.

Discreetly infiltrating humankind on our planet,
Embarrassingly, it is stripping us of
   advancement.
Weakening integrity, honor, and growth,
Dividing the members and removing hope.

Like an impairing disease,
Bringing society to its knees,
It has wildly circulated throughout the masses.
Wasting time and causing them to be obsessive.

A betrayal that creates unexpected challenges
  for good truth upholders,
Which are witnessing the purging of their careers
  and positions as leaders.
The bulk sat back willingly, watching it be done,
Disrespecting the supremacy of the tongue.

Supporting those who have climbed the Liars'
  Tower,
Cheering them on, helping them to influential
  power.
Electing to embrace that which is the illusion,
Intensifying strength of the many delusions.

Pursuing the limited security in perceived power
  founded in false egoistic pretenses.
Overlooking that truth is always required in
  order to move beyond the present.
Degrading honesty has become a most common
  and supported value.
Striving to make certain that there is no chance
  of an ethical future.

What type of tomorrow is there for anyone in
  falseness?
Unless to victimize earth and ourselves in more
  entrapments.

Consistently riddled in horror and secrets in the
  need to be the controlling victor.
Historically, the profitable agendas are clear, it is
  an accurate predictor.

This escalates double-talk and hampers
  standards that only lead to more controls,
Ensuring continued freedom for themselves in
  following their own selfish set of rules.
The clutches of rottenness are wide-spread
And in fear that others are a similar threat.

Strategically setting the human race up to
  succumb to only *them*.
Resulting in an emotionless and mechanical fate
  that condescends.
Domineering artificial intelligence and
  regulations meant to manage us,
Intrusively guaranteeing that only we are
  individually verified worthy to trust.

It has been happening in various forms for eons.
Repeating history with the same attainments.
It impedes people from discovering how innately
  powerful
And compelling our lives can be when living
  authentically truthful.

Universal order intends to help human's move
   forward from birth.
It is based in honesty, kindness, and the earning
   of self-worth.
Light guides freedom, balanced by diversity and
   connectivity.
It embraces curiosity, trust, faith, and raises
   creativity.

Darkness is unsteadily polarized with many
   undisclosed and harsh limitations
(Which is why it prefers to interfere through
   micro-managing and facilitation).
Being true, matures reality within the soul,
Advancing each individually, then as a whole.

Embodying this flourishing view is a light burst
In how to increase humanities overall worth.
Where like-action and intent foster fulfilling
   known and unknown desires;
Threatening the stability of the tower and totally
   terrifying all the towers liars!!!

THE LOVER'S SCOPE

The lovers are of great passion, equality, and
   devotion,
Where heads and hearts unite in corresponding
   motion.
Illustrated through the beauty in forms of art as
   in; literature, music, or nature.
All sharing a kind and understanding kinship that
   develops the skill of nurture.

Genuine in appreciation, gratefulness, and
   honesty.
All mixing the mind's logic with the heart's
   generosity.

Intentional gestures of affection and non-
  judgment will soften resistance.
Using compassion, will provide a safe place for
  resolving reluctance.

Common sense and caring are the paths to loves
  clarity and expertise.
They result in gaining optimistic stillness,
  calmness, and inner peace.
Love thrives in ongoing celebration from this
  sweetest form of friendship,
By choices that increase health, spiritual
  devotion, selflessness, and partnership.

If these qualities are imbalanced, it will drain and
  be overwhelming.
Encouraging the superficial side of the ego in
  being domineering.
Misrepresenting so that sickly obsession and
  impulsiveness excel,
Damaging to the mental, physical, spiritual, and
  self-image health.

Whereupon external comparing overpowers self-
  esteem,
Attaching it to a quickly inflated delusional
  extreme.

Provoking emotions of overburdening and
  resentfulness.
Trust wanes, love collapses, and it fortifies
  bitterness.

Of the two extreme ranges above,
What say you about your life with love?
Are each 'thought' and action strengthening or
  weakening this obtainable goal?
For these are the only holistic writers that can
  expand and evolve the lover's scope.

MAGICAL DATING MATURITY

Charming, thrilling and enchanting.
Aspiring to see sacredness in all things.
Intense life-events instill the fear of being
 misunderstood,
Bravely set aside in the belief that humankind is
 primarily good.

With courage and wisdom, one can advance,
Facing the challenges created by circumstance.
It encourages all to identify with the beliefs of
 invincibility,
Where all things, even love, are within
 possibility.

Simply believing in the inability to evolve,
 inhibits and causes one to regress.
Not learning from the darker sides, will strangle
 the miraculous and depress.
Growth and action are then not be applied,
By favoring a fantasy, things get cockeyed.

It is a choice to forget that thought, intention
 and actions,
Spark natural kinetic manifestations toward
 attraction!
If the magic of love exists in your spiritual
 swagger;
Healthfully maturing it to first, will really help to
 make it matter.

MEALTIME PARTNERSHIP

This world can be such a confusing place.
Life supports life in this Universal space.
The need to consume other life-forms
Is confusing as to why this is the norm.

I am humbled and grateful for what sustains my
  own life.
With appreciation, it supports and forever
  becomes a part of mine.
I am still learning to honor this relationship,
By taking good care of this physical mastership.

Life in its many forms is diverse and different.
It does not matter if we fully understand.
This partnership in survival is based on respect
  and a shared dependence,
Available only as long as we do not waste this
  important hearty balance.

MEET MY COLORED SEAT

Many people are impaired by extreme light or
  dark.
This two-choice world is politically nothing but a
  farce.
Controlling with self-importance, justifying the
  callus and unrefined,
Where different becomes exploited, invisible or
  unrecognized.

Not connecting that many, created and got me
  here;
Of every color, size, and shape, all have been
  very dear.
Oh, wait! A freckled bottom designed my
  silhouette?
Please, send me back, refuse, as this is totally
  incorrect.

Ignoring, you plop on seats made by another
  race.
Really, I am asking, what difference does it
  make?
You need a chair – so you really do not care.
A superficial position in need of great repair.

Quickly forgetting this ludicrous human
  ineptitude.
Readily exchanging it for comfort and quick
  gratitude.
Effortlessly perching a center crack upon my
  seat.
Never contemplating what happens when we
  meet:

It matters not to me how pricey your covers.
A clean and concealed end is never a bother.
Disruptive eruptions are certainly feared silent
  enemies.
But above all; wear underwear before sitting on
  me.

There is no person's bum that is cheekier than
  the rest.
Even a chair knows what all comes out of the
  very best.

Arrogant, egoic, superficial, and lazy as a thought
  can be,
To think that I am as stupid about the color
  sitting on me.

Fluffy air is all this is, caused by a false identity.
Conforming to a silly, mistaken, fake superiority.
An emotionally shallow and destructive craving
Where money is the factor fighting its breaking.

I do not care if you are black, yellow, green,
  purple, seen, or unseen.
Nor about the hail bumps forming or the lengthy
  split of your seam.
Under each bottom I can inform,
That there is clearly a need to reform.

THE MONEY ME ILLUSION

We live in a world where most all are completely
  fooled
By those above everyone, hidden in a secret
  pool.
Placing sturdy puppet strings around our necks,
With a stronghold goal of controlling our wallets.

They live worshipping the following Profit
  Security formula most vehemently:
Consistent + Predictable + Controllable Profits =
  A Secure Formula in Profitability.
Where extremes can spread untouched, fueled
  by the lack of ethical and moral scruples,
Insatiably crumbling and diverting others money
  or materials, not caring how very cruel.

Greed in all its destructive glory is more than a
  human trait for sure.
The question for our kind is: "How much more
  do we choose to endure?"
It all gets so confusing, which is the way it is
  designed.
Openly pointing fingers to keep us distracted and
  totally blind.

Altering and twisting former and present facts is
  a most heinous crime.
Shattering our faith and trust in each other and
  nobility, yet another time.
It also motivates fright that turns us all into
  confused human saps,
Fueling both sides with drama; making it
  impossible to unwrap.

Pitting everyone against each other makes it
  easy to keep people preoccupied.
Insuring the impenetrable ceiling is far away
  from unwanted and inquisitive eyes.
Carefully covering and collaborating scripts with
  just enough truth bent,
To undermine wisdom and seriously challenge
  our basic common sense.

Selfishly engineered to cause trauma and
  hopelessness,
To keep most unevolved in never ending
  changelessness.
Stimulating passivity in perpetual cycles of
  delusion.
Altering truth with carefully crafted and
  executed illusion.

Producing calamities with and without nature in
  numbers greater than before.
As event after event, further discloses the
  ulterior of the masked and obscure.
Historically numbing and restraining; explicitly
  scheming to remove our greatest gifts in life:
Freedom and emotion; where creativity, passion,
  and success flourish, keeping us connected,
  curious, and alive.

It is immense, widespread, and systematically
  dissolves individual power.
Persuading all in how to think about what and
  whomever we might encounter.
Hiding secure and unseen, safe behind powerful
  and protective desks.
Easily fooling us over the course of time, we
  could have never guessed.

It is not more weapons that we need,
But the entire truth to come with speed.
Whatever it is that we all discover,
Is better by far than keeping it undercover.

Knowledge has been rigorously hoarded, tucked
away in deceiving places, and concealed from
all.
Truth is now trickling out of this shadowy veil;
inherently, we knew one day it would come to
call.
Ravenously self-serving, as this also removes all
that is dear, sustaining a world that is all about
controller's and not we.
Crippling this planet in malignant suffering, to
improve stature and to further heap their
"money me."

Motives are rarely completely crystal clear,
foreseen, or fully imagined.
Much has been masked in order to mislead in
such a fruitful fashion.
Those entangled should step up and share that
which is secret, and bring what is known out.
We wish to determine truth for ourselves, to
engage, and to help turn things about.

This is the pinnacle, where honesty begins to
  unfold layers of deceit.
Exposing the ultimate betrayals that we must
  stand up and defeat.
All this will forever alter the world we thought
  we have or had.
Please, do not be tempted to turn away,
  disengaging in dread.

We must face the corruption that is darkening
  quality and replaying the past.
This is not the first-time human beings have
  been deceived, and likely not the last.
Let us embrace ancient Universal guidance to aid
  the struggle of humankind.
Filtering and acting through a loving heart are
  the way to release current binds.

They are seeking the vast riches that are
  stashed away within each human heart.
Deep from a sacred place, where the supreme
  power of emotion sets us apart.
It is the most sought after, dynamic, and
  precious human attribute of all.
We cannot afford to ignore these thieves any
  longer, or again we shall fall.

Elect now to begin participating in this expansion
  of human-deliverance,
Clearing away deceptions, rebuilding intellect
  and reconnecting collective sense.
Unite to blend past and present truths, to begin
  liberating the world we live in.
Courageously saving this shared home, being
  methodically undermined from within.

NATURE'S NUTRITION

Let's get inspiration from nutrition!
A sensible step in healthful volition.
Nature has made the perfect foods,
But manipulation has got us screwed.

Even the word food no longer has value.
So much is just fake, refined, and hallow.
It no longer is able to support our system,
So, illness and disease have little resistance.

The physical is only a small part of this equation,
As the body and energy do not thrive on
  imitation.
Each cell within the body is 90% energy,
Proven by science researching *synergy.

It sickens, drains, and lessens the divine,
As energy too needs nourishment to survive.
Natural nutrition carry's this energetic food.
It is required, unseen, and incredibly astute.

Carefully choose what is put into the mouth!
For each can alter present and future health.

Refuse cloned or faux food and regain some
  control.
Elevate health by deciding to be nutritionally
  bold.

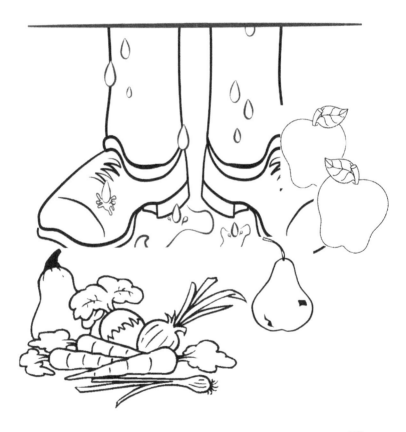

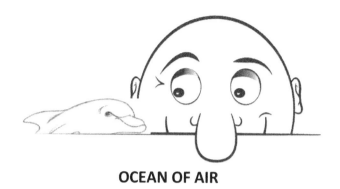

OCEAN OF AIR

In observing wild animals, it is wise to just watch.
Not to interfere, distract, and not to touch.
This behavior is as old as all creatures,
And is the most incredible of teachers.

Like the oceans of water packed with life,
Our ocean of air, is just as full and alive.
The animals observe what we cannot see
And do not interfere in the roles of such things.

Humanity has never been here alone,
Others are involved without being known.
Physical or not they live beyond our gaze
This is not new, it has always been this way.

The unseen, are just as varied as visible life can
  be.
A realm with both positive and negative energy.

Each can have an impact on life, as some feed off negative human energetic nutrients to meet their needs.

This is why it is imperative to know how to tell which voice is yours and which are not within our heads.

THE TEACHER THAT DARED TO SHARE

In school there was a teacher,
Who sang and played a guitar.
Peaking in me, unknown deep desires,
Circulating her love hour after hour.

She was such a breath of fresh air
Always showing the power of care.
Teaching the beauty of the heart.
Surrendering herself and her art.

Thank you for all you shared,
As few others could compare.
So, in my hands I took
A guitar and music book.

Escaping life in the tones and the songs,
I found a voice, and felt I belonged.
Pushing the boundaries of the norm,
A woman was eventually formed!

Thank you Miss Jurgens

TODAY I LIVED AND DIED

In this twenty-four-hour day,
I am not sure what to say.
My body is unsettled and worn,
<u>83</u> years from the day I was born.

Hopeful, I began a physical life,
Superb and yet full of strife.
Challenging me all of the way,
Right up to this very last day.

"Emotion travels with people beyond the grave,"
  they say.
"So, please, be careful, do not waste this
  precious last day.
Review only love in this fading life that was led.
Embrace the detachment of existence thread."

There is much beauty and healing in this
  moment between two worlds.
A light, soft fog gently encircles me, soothingly it
  loosens my stronghold.
My body feels warm, relaxed, all very familiar, I
  can be adaptable,
Letting go of resistance to now release myself
  from self-imposed-obstacles.

I look around the room, there are familiar and
  loving earthly faces.
It is so very humbling and comforting to be
  joined here of all places.
I know each of you from times in this life of great
  joy and sadness,
Together we roamed in a world burdened with
  madness.

The physical and mental shackles are now
  broken,
Boundaries removed and nothing forgotten.
My rising spirit freely moves without the barriers
  of physical form.
Traditional with the exit routes before, things
  begin to transform.

Etheric family and friends join in this day I have
  lived and died,
They gently fetch and bring me safely to the
  other side.
My spirit is surprisingly lovelier than I ever
  imagined.
It is the most stunning thing, impossible to have
  envisioned.

Life at all levels is astonishingly magnificent.
It is connections, participation, and evolvement.
Joining with the frequencies of penetrating grace
  and peace that surrounds.
On this extraordinary day, I have lived and left,
  heaven bound.

VIBRATIONAL MOONING
(Prayer/Meditation to reveal life's main purpose)

I wish upon the bright lunar shining light;
To reveal my life's goal by next moon's night.
So ancient, mysterious, and often inspiring.
Gently share this life's intended enlightening.

Calm and chaotic energies organize and begin to
  move, churn, and flow.
Instantly responding and combining in the
  moon's familiar and time-honored glow.
This night, this day, this month, this year;
The change I want to see is nearly here.

Constraints are gone and I am ready for my
  principal journey to begin.
Committing to its purpose and seeing it all the
  way through to the end.

Quieting the mind, just witnessing; clarity begins
  to bubble up from inside of me.
Shedding deceptions and expanding
  consciousness, fosters the best version I can be.

Blending intentional uplifting spirit with the
  moon's authoritative power,
Generates receptiveness and the capacity to
  manifest positive desires.
Connecting like roots to heaven and earth
  sustains the inner-being, providing solid ground
  for standing on in life.
Integrate this with creative and inspiring energy,
  then blend it all with the moon's encouraging
  and fortifying light.

Its glow and power penetrate everything; every
  thought, flesh and bone.
Combining dynamic, timeless, ordered energy
  with the perfect vibrational tone.
Courageous with faith and trust, setting all
  unhealthy fear aside,
Relinquishing control and bravely letting the life-
  force be the guide.

Softly brighten the way and simplify for me how:
To bring that without, within, to merge with the
  now.

Meticulously guide me towards the dreams I can
  scarcely dare to dream.
Where pure essence and the physical fuse into
  the universal stream.

Instantly, I am seeing clearly before me a vaguely
  remembered hall.
With large heavy doors and soft lanterns, the
  shapes of balls.
Challenges are captive here, they are the
  building blocks of human growth.
Strive hard to work through and complete
  whatever this place makes known.

From the smallest spark of a thought inside the
  head,
To an overwhelming and difficult hall that one
  might dread.
Each forward step taken, brings about
  advancement,
And breaks down hindering defensive human
  resistance.

Others have come down this hall before,
Accepting the excursion to transform.
The opening doors are rarely meant just for one.
All must work together for progress to be won.

Gratitude rises for others helping to clear away
  pitfalls.
As this unclutters the room making it easier to
  face for all.
Every chamber reveals lessons, masters, mentors
  and teachers within.
Near the brilliant and densest corners of each
  space is where to begin.

This is a perpetuating school with many lifetimes
  of countless mistakes towards progression.
Adapting, exploring, participating, and redefining
  are repeated many times for this evolution.
I am ready now, to discover the rooms within
  life's main objective.
Explicitly reveal them now, as I am ultimately
  most receptive.

Tenderly, clearly, divulge to me, the goal of this
  life's longest hallway.
With an unobstructed view, where others have
  helped eased the way.
Ensure I do not miss the message, and that I
  accurately remember it,
And do this please; before the close of the next
  glorious moon-lit night.

THE "WHAT BLAH"

A nonsensical hogwash world to live in,
Intent on removing the real and genuine.
Supportive of all that we believe is dear
To only find out, it was mostly not real.

Concealed, is a "What Blah" to promote
  undermining dreams,
Addicting and hypnotizing, it lives through
  technology screens.
Compromising health while blankly staring to
  dull the brain,
Emptying, numbing, and rewiring it until nearly
  drained.

Totally immersed in elaborate fiddle-faddle,
Instigating many a personal and public battles.

Rubbish in, results in rubbish kabuki,
An ongoing garbage of hooey-balooey.

Burdening the mind with drivel and gibberish.
All because we thoughtlessly push that switch.
Everyone is contaminated; no one goes
  unaffected,
Each person has at least one "What Blah"
  connected.

The "What Blah" is attached to everyone's brain.
We welcomed it, not knowing the loss in its
  gains.
An unseen race within vibrational undertones.
Ensuring that each human mind is owned.

Always nearby, waiting for the opportunity of
  receptivity,
Then quickly entering the host with its deceptive
  negativity.
Masterfully engineering a drowsy, compelling
  trance, where disconnection and inactivity are
  reinforced.
Destroying willing people's ability to commune
  with others, ourselves, and the energy force.

Deep within our own "What Blah" we will find,
That much it implants, is meant to be unkind.

Convincing us to feel, speak, think, and care,
In ways that undermine every vision dared.

Decaying the substructure of most all that has
  been earned.
Altering and eroding with frequency techniques
  they learned,
Persuading each mind to engage in a repeating
  thought-race?
Relentlessly, it blinds us to the guidance of spirit
  already in place.

This is why there is so much unfavorable mind
  chatter?
It is 'blah'-babble creating this unending negative
  jabber.
It is all expertly drafted for manipulating through
  mind interference
From the "What Blah" agenda in costly
  encouragement and influence.

Pride swells within this creature as it suckles on
  unaware minds.
An unseen snipe intended to keep us agreeable
  without knowing its kind.
Step away, focus to excel and evolve beyond,
Learn to seriously develop love for the one.

As this most precious and powerful emotion for
  self,
Contradicts the "What Blah" and puts it on the
  shelf.
Practicing on ourselves first, is how we learn.
Then experienced, we can love others in return.

Technology, used well, has many superior and
  helpful advantages.
Balance it out by turning technology off to
  disrupt its intrusive damages.
Become incompatible with constant self-kind
  thoughts, words, and actions.
This will lead to a strong defensively robust
  barrier to the "What Blah" attraction.

THE ZONE OF THE OFFENDING CODE

When sensing the feeling of offense,
Witness, observe and do not get bent.
It is needed energy bellowing up to be noticed,
Alerting to impairing thoughts through emotion.

A person must be able to define what they are
  feeling.
To be deeply self-aware, as this can be used to
  heighten inner-healing.
These specific emotions are not because of
  someone else,
But is all about what is hiding or denied within
  the self.

This takes commitment, introspection, and
  patience to achieve.
Continually adjusting, healing, and repairing how
  to perceive.

It naturally teaches when and if to surrender,
Aiding in quick adapting to make living easier.

This is the place of clear divine communication
On how and when to make insightful corrections.
It requires awareness, action, attention and is
  not meant just to contemplate and ponder.
There is much here on earth intended to take
  away and stifle human curiosity and wonder.

In time, reflecting about this code will be non-
  existent,
Reaching the prize where answers come in an
  instant.
Society and ourselves play a role in impairing and
  manipulating communications,
Dividing with deception through the creation of
  reality with misleading information.

We are all in need of supportive, truthful, and
  understanding partnerships.
Where there is equality, balance, and a mutual
  give and take fellowship.
So please, give others and yourself a break.
Strive to do what it takes to achieve this state.

Start by letting go of exaggeration and face the
  truths behind acting, feeling, and speaking.
Compassionately critiquing ideas on self-
  limitations, imperfections, and faulty being.
Emotional life-forms all have in common the
  ease of being offended, it is an individualized
  evolutionary gift.
It results in achieving easier states of being that
  manifest life as art, and give it a healthy
  liberating lift.

Build skills in this codes power to bring up
  denied truths.
Be wise in being honest with yourself and others
  first.
This clarifies accuracy, and acceptance of the
  power in the Offending Code.
It will guide self-development, and illuminate life
  in a vigorous yet gentle flow.

Authenticity is the propeller necessary for every
  mental and physical effort.
It will help bypass and break down the
  troublesome contradictions at work.

It is a recipe for taking full responsibility and
  ownership,

By addressing each facet of the self-awareness
  relationship.

This technique modifies thoughts with world
  actuality,
For a more accurate life with less superficiality.
It is an education where you are not failing, you
  are learning through the mistakes made
So next time, things can be approached and
  handled in a much more enlightened way.

No one here is telling anyone how or when to
  act, feel, think, or practice,
I am just sharing what I have found in being an
  Offending Code apprentice.
As a unique expression, only you can find your
  pivotal,
Where the beliefs of life are strong and much
  more livable.

The Offending Code is an elevated level, it is not
  easy at first, but with practice it can be
  achieved.
It is an advancing and empowering skill for any
  expanding, 3rd dimensional being to reach.
Pledging to live this way, is helpful, progressive
  and kind.

It results in a calmer and more nourishing frame of mind.

*DEFINITIONS:

Akashi: The *ether element. Elements are the building blocks for all matter, they are in their purest form. The ether element is the reality that creates distance between points.   It manifest! Akashi is the information we can access and learn from that leads to influencing creation within one's own life and beyond. A Hall-of-Life so to say.   It is part of eternal individual and collective experiences; past, present, and sometimes the outline of the future, but this one is in constant fluctuation.

Align Thinking: When a thought is changed, it cascades throughout all other attitudes/thoughts to show those that must alter to align and balance with the new thinking. Actions and reactions are also meant to align with the new thinking, if they do not then the thought behind such actions must need something changed in order to line-up with the new thought. This is why it is so easy to fall back into past undermining patterns. Each belief will try to align with all others. It is an ongoing process.

Between: Vibrational information for guidance and growth between sound, thought, words, notes, nature, ancestors, life, death, vibration, frequency, and the physical. Is where 2 or more worlds and dimensions meet or overlap. The shore is 3 worlds coming together; ocean, land (above and below), and the cosmos.

Chakras: Energy communication points (72,000 for human beings) within and around the energy of a being or life-form. But the main chakras focused on are the 7 most influential ones from the genitals to the crown on the head. Their vibrational qualities connect to specific organs, systems, thinking, and affects every aspect of health. They send out and take in information and experiences. These can move energy which means their vibrations can be affected by healthier or non-healthier vibration. Accurately defining the changes in a chakra's frequency is one of the languages of the "higher self." This guidance is to support healing and growth through experience. It promotes how a person thinks. Changing thinking, alters energy, and life responds. Its education leads to maintaining well-being in the midst of chaos. Frequency and vibration are a recognized science.

Closed-minded: Those individuals that truly believe their views are the only correct views.

Lacks objectivity, is egoistic, an inability to see other perspectives. These individuals believe that their opinions are absolute. Likely will not even consider proof that the concept is faulty, or be willing to consider any other possibilities. An; "I am right because I think and belief it so" attitude.

Ego: A person's sense of their own importance and value. A healthy ego is one that can honestly take pleasure in others successes, in them having or being more. It needs balance with acceptance and resistance. Unhealthy ego will compare to others where the other person is always, in some form, less than. It will be riddled with insecurities and tries to overcompensate. Ego is a wonderful attribute that has a healthy place in our lives. But it must be kept in check.

The Empty (Emptiness): The essence of energy. On the positive side, it is the place of peace and joy. Where compassion, kindness, humbleness, helpfulness, love, and wisdom all abide in the space of connected grace. It is a frame of mind in one aspect. Each individual is to strive towards this place because it lets go of the chaos outside of ourselves. It is a means of blending with and connecting to that which supports the same, wherever and from whatever that is. All energy is from one beginning; from that 2 sides developed. Ultimately, we blend with until we become part of the divine's energetic essence. In other words – eternity is a very long time, and living lives of learning have an ultimate graduation that is worth seeking if a person wishes to have the choice. Graduation into God's essence rather than continued experience. In life, it is a means of "not sweating the small stuff and living in a way that promotes self-understanding and love so you can do the same with others.

This differs a bit from other translations. It is not empty at all, but a space in which to function from that takes some of the hard out of life. It puts the person in the lead role, for others, the divine, and themselves. It is not selfish to learn how to love and treat yourself with all these principles first. Then we gain some wisdom in how to treat others. Aware that we are a student as the lead role in this life. Watching carefully, observing; for where, when, how, what, and if to participate. It is a form of confidence when spirit becomes the guide. Experience then teaches from different expanding angles. This way of thinking, living, acting, reacting, brings about a multitude of awareness's that lead to vast enlightenment.

One cannot do any of this without the ability to empty thought so the new can come in. this is how to determine what thoughts are really ours, what thoughts are not, and which to listen to. It all takes eternity, lucky us - life.

Energy: Every single cell is 90% energy. Energy creates frequency and vibration that has no boundaries like walls. It is God, spirit, information, the collective, love, compassion, helpfulness or the opposite. Energy creates, mentors and educates. Energy brings to us what we need, and can benefit or block depending on the situation and development of the person or group of beings involved. All life has energy. Spirit requires energetic nutrition to be healthy. This is found in our thinking and in the food that is created by our earth. Our mother in support of life. Energy evolves with nature. There is a point in time where so much has been genetically modified that the energy has no vital nutrients left.

Energy-Flow: There is a rhythm, tone, and movement to energy. When it flows well with life, life becomes easier. Sit next to an angry person, and you can feel it communicating itself. Energy is creation and, it will expand and attract. When working against the flow, it pushes back; work with, it then flows. The metaphor is "pushing against a pull door."

Enlightened: More modern attitudes of connection,   self-responsibility,   diverse   in worldly and spiritual beliefs, continued striving towards self-development and the ability to live at peace in a broader existence that includes the earth and our universe. An understanding of the relationships of the physical and spiritual. Enlightening is ever occurring; that which is known today can totally alter what was known before. It is the knowledge and the connections within all things.   It is removing our inhibiting thinking.   An acceptance of past and present truths. It is seeing beyond that which we are told.   An   awareness   that   comes   from determining truth for ourselves!

Ether (Etheric) Element: The 5th element (air, water, earth, fire, and ether) is the element of the spiritual, the energy of creation. This is the subtlest of the elements. It is the essence of emptiness, is the divine Akashi energy of spirit. It is believed that this is the space in which all life eventually returns. This is also the space within. When our Biorhythms (measured energy that has a reoccurring pattern like sleep) are in line with all the elements, it brings greater balance and connection to the cosmic. It is where Universal knowledge can be accessed. Orbs (Beings that have chosen to bring information from the Ether to human beings – such as a spiritual person seeing a head of a departed one – floating heads are often Orbs) aid in this communication and are positive. They will bring knowledge if asked. Best if you ask to only have those available come. They are busy and love to help so stating this is respectful.

Expansion: To become greater than, in all directions. Those expanded enough ascend, in time, beyond this earth's limitations. It is just the order of things, is ongoing.

Feeling(s):   Energetic/vibration and physical sensations that clue a person into labeled emotions, which contain information about others, the environment or ourselves. It is a means to better understanding energetic communication from within and beyond.

God: Whether it is a single particle of energy, or a full-blown concept of a human looking God, it is the same.   All that matters are that God/Spirit/Energy/Vibration/I Am/Great Spirit... is creation, connection, and knowledge. It was there at the beginning and nothing else was, we cannot be separate from the creator. Divinity expands and learns from the experiences all life offers both seen and unseen. Other beings are just as confused as we, so do NOT fall for them portraying themselves as a God. The God I speak of is the one and only original God. To me it is based in essence of pure love. Of course, in a dual Universe, both extremes exist.

Grace: Patience, humility, gentleness, kindness, forgiveness, gratefulness, embodies balance and pure love, is knowing when to and when not to control. Is compassion, emotion (as I just cannot see that beings without emotion having the ability to reach grace), wisdom, ability to connect, excellence and respect for self and environment, confidence… Moments being in grace's presence, participating with grace, is worth striving for. It is human and spiritual excellence.

Heal: Working towards reasonable optimum mental, spiritual, and physical health. This can only be accomplished by facing the truth within ourselves, the environment, and by accurately communicating, acting, and reacting to the guidance we get from all these areas.   It is aligning thinking, emotions, feelings, actions, and reactions that serve us rather than sabotage. To correct disease, illness, structural damage, mental instability, and energy imbalance.

Higher-Self: This is partly the sub-conscious mind (has all experiences, can be influenced by outside sources; is where communication can go beyond the physical human experience). It also embodies our 2nd brain – the digestive system. We have many parts of our spirit that can be busy elsewhere, simultaneously so the higher self can get guidance in for this life and for another part in a different life. Our higher self is our guide and reference point. It is our direct vibrational communication source to information in the ether.

Kinetic (Kinesiology): Kinetic energy is energy in motion. Energy's potential lies dormant until it awakens.   There are 3 types of energy; electricity, magnetics, and electromagnetics. These break down into further energy categories.   In this context, as electrons flow, they generate electricity or heat. Electrons can move in many different directions and take on many mediums.   Magnetic energy causes like and wanted energy to be attracted to it as well as sending messages out. Like feeling that angry person next to you, again. This is how energy healing works. The magnetic, moving energy, grab's onto other energy and brings it in to heal and balance its own. It also releases unwanted energy but requires replacement energy. Again, this is how energy healing works.   Energy in Kinesiology is also a form of communication. The energy of the muscles and skeleton weaken with negative and strengthen with positive and is called 'muscle testing' when being used to get answers of yes and no for whatever is needed. This has an absolute impact on our health and well-being. However, this is a skill that most are not educated enough to be doing. It is rare to find someone that knows anything about the need to check and reset the energy so the answers are accurate. There are boundaries and energetic needs that must be met. Check the website at www.holisticcollaboration.com for a future class in the necessary skills of kinesiology testing.

Light: The frequency and vibrational energy of grace; the pure love and compassion in thinking, actions, and reactions. The power of light to penetrate the darkness. It is ethical and respectful of life. It is the God of love, for me, and support with everyone's best interest at heart regardless of the maneuvering of others.

Love: A strong feeling of affection for another. It is supportive of healthiness in a close relationship. If healthy, it is respectful, has genuine admiration, and has the other persons back, is non-judgmental, in support of reasonable actions, considers the other, is kindness and friendship first. Seeing the beauty in the soul of other life, and within the self. Love is binding in actions and words. Is safe, balanced, and is wise. It is compassionate connection.

Manifestation: What we think and how we choose to participate with what helps to create our experiences and ultimately will bring about our deepest desires. It is lining up emotion, feeling, and thinking with the true essence of the heart. Manifestation occurs with all thinking. The more like-mindedness the greater the impact manifestation can have. It is creation and fruition of thinking, actions, and reactions.

Sociopathic: A person void of some if not all emotions. Often overcompensating with one or two such as love and anger. This type of thinking is similar to the addicts thinking by becoming seasoned in lying, omitting, manipulating, and selfishness. They are all about what they are after and want.   Many times, sabotaging themselves in the long run. They will risk life. (A psychopath does not lose and can risks lives beyond that of their target. Never considering the broad effects of their actions on others.) Both damage relationships.   There are very specific criteria to meet in order to be properly classified as a sociopath or psychopath. Both learn how to respond so as to hide the emotional voids. I suggest reading 5 quality books on each if you wish to have a generally accurate understanding. Both are either born this way, or become this way due to the environment (trauma). Addiction brings out symptoms of these personalities and disconnects people from their emotions, as well as, causes the individual to be extremely vulnerable to negative seen and unseen influencers.

Soul: The part of you that is your mind, character, thoughts, and feelings. It is the whole of the individual. All parts here or elsewhere come together to make the whole. Some choose to live several lives at the same time. We do not know our whole until we die and go through transition where we reconnect with the other parts of us learning elsewhere. It is the total essence, the energetic form of beings.

Surrender(ing): The art of letting go of expectations and letting spirit be the guide. Complete trust and faith in the direction and experiences that arise. It is knowing when to let go of control, and when to take control. When complete surrender is achieved, great creativity occurs. It is the essence of faith and trust. A giving into guidance and moving forward as spirit directs. In the physical plane it may be simply choosing to step back and let someone else be in charge or to change direction immediately when one is not working. A releasing of resistance, being in the present, and participating in whatever way supports others and the situation.

Synergy: Energy gathers, combines, and has a cause and effect. It is a collaboration of energy, a working together of like and different energies/molecules/particles. The effects are always greater when combined. Strength in numbers. This can also mean a pulling together of physical items such as companies, intending to combine for a larger impact and result. The intent is energy and results in the combining of energy, thought, goals...

Well-being: Overall mental, physical, spiritual, and life health. Is joyful and peaceful life balance. Confidently trusting in the ability to handle whatever. It is balanced thinking with supportive actions and reactions. It is joyful, honest, aware, and peaceful. When emotion is used as a guide and not the lead. The ability to change thinking to fit the circumstance. It is whatever requires healing to be done so that functioning in multiple realities becomes easier.

Sherry Bainbridge PhD, is a Naturopath, Hypnotherapist, Medical/Spiritual Intuitive, and Reiki Master/Teacher. With self-education, formal education, client experiences, and personal experiences in both the physical and spiritual realms; Sherry truly is an original and has gained a unique perspective of life. She will stay connected through her Holistic Collaboration series YouTube show; "Peeves, Tips, and Tricks", and her website at:

www.holisticcollaboration.com

A note from Sherry:
Thank you so much for reading this book. I do hope you enjoyed the poems. I really look forward to hearing your thoughts.

Thank you beautiful person,
Sherry

WHAT THEY ARE SAYING ABOUT SHERRY

Sherry Bainbridge attended the funeral/memorial service and wake of my sister. She shared things that there was no way she could have known. She was spot on and very comforting. She has a knack for inserting just the right amount of humor and a laughter that is very healing. The coroner, a few weeks later, confirmed exactly what Sherry had stated. Sherry is gifted and genuine. *Katheryn K.* Thornton, Colorado

Just wanted to take a moment to thank you for the hypnotherapy session. It was a life-changing experience. Thank you for introducing me to the Angels and for being part of my healing journey. Love, *Laura B.* Aurora, Colorado

It was extremely powerful meeting with you today. Having been trained in "the hard sciences" and was very skeptical of the holistic approach. Well, as you said, while laughing; "you are very stubborn" – quite right! You have managed to do that which people have attempted to do for decades. I am energized, clear and very happy. Your demeanor, intelligence, and compassion are greatly appreciated. I am going to follow your instructions explicitly and live a better life. Best regards, *Jim F.* Aurora, Colorado

Many thank you's for the terrific Hypnotherapy and Reiki healing sessions. An old unsightly scar on my leg cleared up shortly after the first session. Ugly discolorations around my ankles have completely cleared up, and my dry hands have returned to looking younger and smoother. I am also sleeping much better. You're Great! *Pat S.* Los Angeles, California

Thank you, Sherry. 5 months ago, I was rushed to the hospital and the MRI showed 5 kidney stones. The doctors assured me they were coming out. I drank the tea as you suggested. Every time I went to the bathroom, I was expecting the worst and nothing happened. After 6 weeks not one sign of kidney stones. Seriously, thanks. After your hypnosis treatment and nutrition consultation my acid reflux has completely cleared up after 30 years of struggling with it. Thanks again, *Nick B.* Idaho Falls, Idaho

Sherry, I have made many changes in my life after your consultation. I did move to Florida and as you had said, I am very happy. Thank you for opening my mind, showing me a different way to think, and helping me find the courage to live my dream. You are a gift Sherry. Thanks, *Ronald M.*, Pennsylvania

Made in the USA
Middletown, DE
22 July 2023

35496871R00060